BARKIS

BARKIS

Story and Pictures by
CLARE TURLAY NEWBERRY

SMITHMARK

This edition published in 1998 by SMITHMARK Publishers, a division of
U.S. Media Holdings, Inc., 115 West 18th Street, New York, NY 10011.

SMITHMARK books are available for bulk purchase for sales promotion
and premium use. For details write or call the manager of special sales,
SMITHMARK Publishers, 115 West 18th Street, New York, NY 10011;
212-519-1300.

Library of Congress Catalog Card Number: 97-62213
ISBN: 0–7651–9056–7

Printed in Hong Kong
10 9 8 7 6 5 4 3 2 1

To my Mother and Father

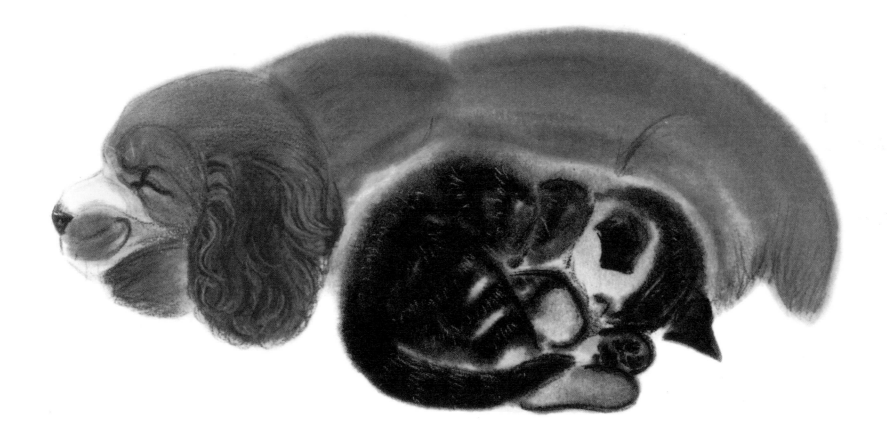

BARKIS

JAMES' ninth birthday had been fun. Just being nine years old at last was something, besides all the excitement of opening gifts. There was a Young Chemist's set from his father, a sweater from his mother, a silver dollar from his grandma, and a book about Indians from Nell Jean, his sister, who was ten-and-a-half and very fond of reading.

Then, too, there was the lovely cake his mother had baked for him, with pink icing on it, and HAPPY BIRTHDAY in green squiggles across the top. So James should have been very happy.

And he was, really. Only he felt a little sad, too, the way you cannot help feeling when you have had all your gifts and it is nearly bedtime and you know you won't have another birthday for a whole long year.

He sighed as he fingered the big round dollar in his pocket. Once more he raised the lid of his Young Chemist's set, to admire its rows of mysterious little bottles. He would have liked to see the pictures in his new book, too, but Nell Jean was already reading that, curled up in an armchair, with Edward, her striped kitten, purring on her shoulder.

Suddenly a car stopped in front of the house. A loud beeeeeeeeeep-beep-beeeeep sent Edward scampering under the sofa.

"It's Uncle Jimmy!" shouted James, and he raced out of the house.

When he reached the car his uncle was lifting a large box out of the back seat. It was a brown pasteboard carton, tied with heavy cord, and there were holes about as big as a lead-pencil punched here and there in its sides.

"What is it, Uncle Jimmy? What is it?" begged James. "Is it for me? Is it, Uncle Jimmy?"

"You just wait and see!" laughed his uncle. He carried the box into the house and set it on the floor. Then he said, "Happy birthday, James! Go ahead—open it!"

The whole family gathered round to see what was in the box—all except Edward, who felt safer watching from under the sofa. Even Nell Jean put down her—I mean *James'*—book and came to see what Uncle Jimmy had brought.

James frowned importantly as he got his jackknife out of his pocket and tugged open a blade. He sawed through the heavy cords, then quickly lifted the flaps of the carton and looked inside.

What he saw was so wonderful that he simply stared.

In the bottom of the box, peering anxiously up at him, sat a small, solemn, brown puppy. His short tail began to wag when he saw James, but his dark eyes remained anxious and pleading.

"*Boy!*" breathed James, and he picked up the puppy and hugged him close.

The puppy lay quite still at first, while James softly stroked his plushy back and his small sleek head. But pretty soon he began to poke his cold nose into James' neck, making happy snuffling noises.

"He likes me, Daddy! He really does!" cried James joyfully. "He's snoofing in my neck like anything. *Ooh! he tickles!*"

"His name is Barkis," beamed Uncle Jimmy, "and he's a cocker spaniel."

"Well, he sure is a swell dog," said James, turning his face to escape the puppy's wet tongue. "Thanks, Uncle Jimmy—thanks an *awful* lot!"

"He's just darling, Uncle Jimmy," cried Nell Jean, letting Barkis nibble her finger tips with his little sharp teeth. "Just feel how soft his ears are, Mamma! And look, they're *natural curly!* Oh, I just love him! Is he part mine, Uncle Jimmy?"

"*No!*" yelled James, before his uncle could answer. "He's all mine, isn't he, Uncle Jimmy? He's my own birthday dog, isn't he?"

Uncle Jimmy looked startled.

"Why, yes, of course," he said uneasily. "But you will share him with your sister, won't you, James?"

"Of course he will," James' father said heartily. "You want Nell Jean to play with the puppy, too, don't you, son?"

A stubborn look had come into James' face.

"Nell Jean's already got Edward," he muttered sulkily, "and she never

12

would let me have any of *him*. So why do I have to give her part of my own birthday dog? It's not fair," said James darkly.

"Children!" said their mother. "What will Uncle Jimmy think of you? Come now, bring the puppy into the kitchen and we'll feed him."

"Oh, that reminds me," said Uncle Jimmy, "you must always feed Barkis out of a cup—not a flat dish—or his 'naturally curly' ears will drag in his dinner." That made the children laugh.

In the kitchen their mother mixed some shredded wheat and milk in a cup and set it on the floor, while the family crowded round to watch Barkis eat.

And how Barkis did eat! He had no table manners whatsoever. With his short legs braced wide apart he lapped fast and noisily. And when he reached the bottom of the cup he licked it so hard that he pushed it all around over the linoleum.

All this time Edward had been hiding under the sofa. But seeing Barkis eat made him feel hungry, too. He crept cautiously from his hiding-place and tiptoed toward the puppy, his ears pricked forward, his whiskers quivering and his round eyes gleaming with excitement.

Barkis, having given the cup one last lick, turned and saw him. For a moment he stood still, his short tail wagging doubtfully, and his babyish forehead wrinkled up in a puzzled frown. Then the hairs bristled along his little back and he growled, "rrrrrrrrrrrr," under his breath.

Suddenly he barked, "Rowf!" and came down playfully on his elbows, with his hind legs still standing up. Edward sat down and eyed him scornfully.

"Rowf!" said Barkis, more bravely this time, and he gave a little bounce and came down again on his elbows, just a trifle closer.

Edward's ears flattened and his kitten tail slowly fluffed out till it looked like a tiny fir tree.

"Fffffffffffff!" he remarked insultingly.

But now Barkis was feeling very brave indeed. He gave a third "Rowf!" and bounced again. Edward's paw shot out.

"Yipe!" squealed Barkis in terror, backing away in a hurry, for the kitten's sharp claws had raked his soft baby nose.

"Mamma!" cried James, "look what that old kitten did! He ought to be ashamed!"

"Never mind," said his mother soothingly. "Barkis and Edward will be good friends when they know each other better. And now you children must go to bed."

So James and Nell Jean each gave Barkis a last lingering hug, and trudged slowly up the stairs. When they were in their beds Nell Jean called to her brother from across the hall:

"Oh, James!"

"What?"

"James, listen," she said coaxingly. "How would you like to trade half of Barkis for half of Edward? Okay?"

"NO!" roared her brother indignantly.

"Aw, *please*, James!" she begged. "Why not?"

"No, *sir!*" said James fiercely. "Why should I want part of your old kitten when I've got a swell new dog all to myself? Dogs are better than cats, anyhow. Everybody knows that."

"They are not!"

"Sure they are. Cats are dumb. Cats can't do tricks the way dogs can."

"They could if they wanted to," cried Nell Jean hotly. "They just don't

want to. So there!"

"That's what *you* say," jeered her brother.

"Well, it's true," declared Nell Jean, close to tears. "Cats are about a million times better than dogs, any day!"

"Aw, they are not." "*They are, too!*" "They are not." "*Are, too!*" "Are not." "*Are!*" "Aren't." "ARE!"

There was a swift step in the hall and both children fell silent.

19

"You children must go right to sleep now," said their mother, and she kissed them each good-night. Then she closed the doors between their two rooms and went back downstairs.

"All the same, dogs *are* better than cats. Everybody knows that," murmured James as he fell asleep.

"I don't care!" sobbed Nell Jean angrily, "I'd rather have Edward than all the old puppies in the whole world! I *hate* dogs!" And burrowing her nose in the pillow, she cried herself to sleep.

WHEN James came in from school the next day Barkis met him at the door, wagging joyfully and bouncing up to lick at his bare knees. He was too frisky to be petted, however, and when James tried to catch him he just barked saucily and scampered out of reach.

With a gleeful whoop James was after him, and they chased each other merrily around the room. Then James stumbled over a scuffed-up rug, and fell to the floor in a laughing heap. At once Barkis was on top of him, licking his face, nipping his ears, and tugging at his clothes and hair, all the while growling delightedly.

"You win!" gasped James. He shook the puppy loose and, flushed and

tousled, struggled to his feet. "You wait here, Barkis," he said. "I'm going upstairs to get my ball."

He remembered seeing the ball under his bed that very morning. But it wasn't there now. His mother had picked it up and put it in the toy-box, where it belonged. And as he looked everywhere else first, he did not find it for some time.

Nell Jean had come in quietly while James and the puppy were playing, and had settled herself by the window to read. She had made up her mind to pay no attention to mean old James and his puppy. So when little Barkis, feeling lonely with James upstairs, nibbled softly at her shoelace, she just drew her feet up haughtily beneath her and went on reading.

Barkis watched her hopefully for a moment, his head on one side, and his eyes wistful. But she did not look up, so he trotted to the screen-door and stared out, sniffing the fresh air. He propped his fore paws against the door, and to his surprise it swung slowly open with him, and he landed on all fours on the porch.

Nell Jean glanced up when she heard the door slam. She wondered if Barkis was old enough to be outdoors by himself. Then she scowled.

"Let James take care of his own old dog," she thought spitefully, and she tried to go on reading.

Barkis sniffed the air eagerly. Trotting to the edge of the porch steps, he peered over. They must have looked very steep to him, for he pattered back and forth at the top, whimpering softly. Presently he started down, very slowly, plop . . . plop . . . plop, his long ears just brushing each step as he went down to it.

At last he reached the cement walk at the bottom, and with a happy little bark he scampered out on the lawn and rolled over and over in the grass.

In spite of herself, Nell Jean glanced out of the window, just in time to see him scramble to his feet, shake his ears, and jog gaily toward the street. She scowled again and bent her gaze upon the book; but it was no use—she just could not read it. She looked out again, and this time no puppy was in sight. Nothing but the empty lawn, and the bare sidewalk, and beyond it the tall green grass that grew along the creek.

Nell Jean gave a little shriek and, flinging down her book, ran out of the house. She clattered down the steps, and a moment later was kneeling beside the creek, pulling a wet and frightened puppy out of the icy water.

"Mamma! Mamma!" she screamed as she rushed back into the house, with Barkis dripping and shivering in her arms.

"Why, what on earth—" began her mother, hurrying to meet her.

"He fell in the creek, Mamma!" panted Nell Jean as her brother, appearing from above with the ball in his hand, stared at Barkis open-mouthed.

"In that cold water!" cried their mother in dismay, taking the shivering puppy. "We must get him warm quickly, before he catches cold. James, you light the gas-heater—quick! Nell Jean, you run out in the hall and get me your old red sweater."

Already she was briskly rubbing the wet puppy with a bath towel, and when the sweater was brought she wrapped him all up in it, so that nothing but his little square muzzle could be seen. Then, drawing up a chair, she held him on her lap before the roaring gas-heater.

"Will he get sick, Mamma?" demanded James anxiously. "I didn't know it hurt puppies to get wet."

"It wouldn't hurt an older puppy," said his mother, "but Barkis is just a baby. He shouldn't even have been bathed for another month. But we'll hope he's all right."

"Would he get *awful* sick, Mamma?" quavered Nell Jean. "Would he . . . I mean, would he get *really* awful sick?"

"We'll hope not, dear," said her mother. "Poor little fellow, he's shivering terribly. James, run and get me your bathrobe. Nell Jean, you go and fill the hot-water bottle. There's hot water in the teakettle."

Soon Barkis had James' woolly bathrobe wrapped about him on top of Nell Jean's old sweater, and a hot-water bottle besides. But he went on shivering just the same. He held very still and good, and did not make a sound, but his soft dark eyes, peering out at them, looked so miserable that Nell Jean began to cry.

"If Barkis dies it will be all my fault," she thought wretchedly.

After what seemed a long time their mother looked up and smiled. "He's not shivering any more, and he's sound asleep," she said cheerfully. "I do believe he's going to be all right. But we must keep him wrapped up until he is entirely dry. Nell Jean, you hold him. I must get dinner."

So Nell Jean held Barkis tenderly, while James, sitting on the floor beside her, clasped one of his pudgy damp paws.

By the time their father came home to dinner Barkis was all dry. And to the joy of everyone, when he was finally unwrapped he was just as good as new. If possible, he was even livelier than before, and the children had a glorious evening romping with him.

That night when they were in bed, James called to his sister. "Nell Jean!"

"What?"

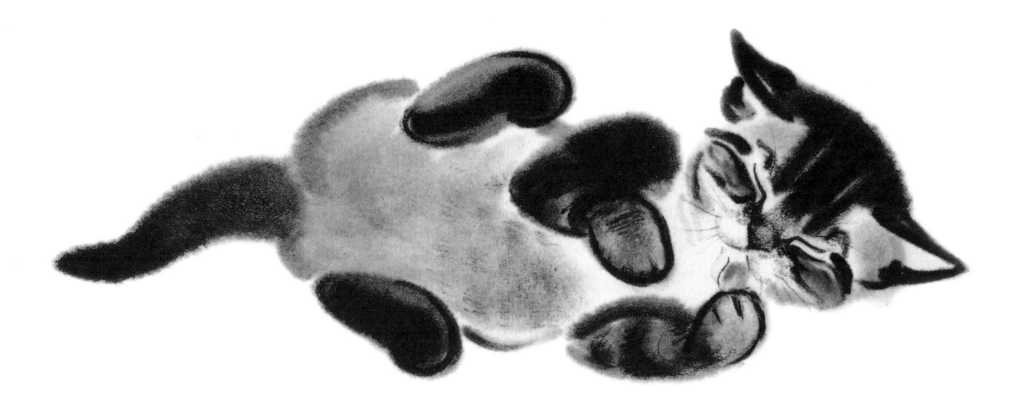

"Say, listen, Nell Jean. If you still want to trade half of Edward for half of Barkis, I guess it's okay. Gosh, you saved his life, practically. I mean, if it hadn't been for you he might have got drowned, or something."

Nell Jean did not answer for a moment. Then she said bravely: "Of course I want to trade. Only . . . I guess *you* won't, if I tell you something."

"What?"

"Well," confessed his sister, "you see, it was my fault he fell in the creek. Because I saw him go outdoors and I didn't stop him, or anything. I didn't think about the creek."

"Oh," said James. "Well, anyway," he said gruffly, "you *did* rescue him. So I guess it's still okay. Anyway, I like Edward an awful lot, too."

Nell Jean was so overcome by his generosity that she could not speak for a few moments. Then she said humbly:

"Look, James, I'll tell you what let's do. I guess Barkis really ought to be mostly yours, on account of your birthday and everything. So let's have it this way: Barkis can be partly mine, but *mostly* yours, and Edward can be partly yours, but *mostly* mine. Okay?"

"*Okay!*" cried James.

Hand-set in Weiss Antiqua type
by Arthur Rushmore and Elaine Rushmore at the
Golden Hind Press, Madison, New Jersey

1938